WHERE DID THEY GO?

a spotting book

Emily Bornoff

In the hot desert, among sand and thorns,

someone is sporting his long, twisted horns.

Where is he hiding? Maybe you know?

Where did the sandy-haired addax go?

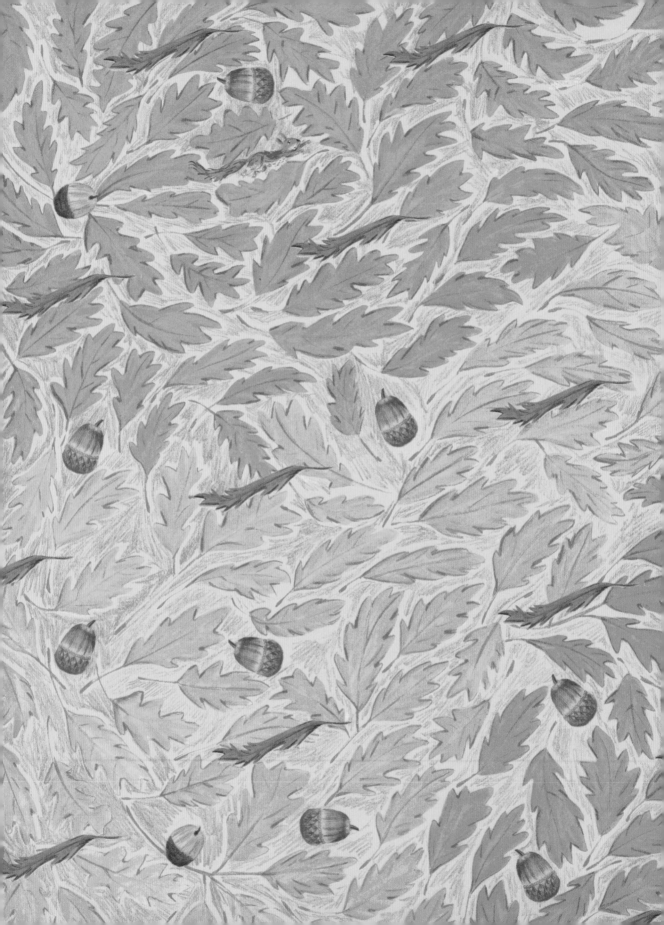

All through the forest, as autumn takes hold,

a creature is dancing through leaves red and gold.

She's looking for acorns to store and to stow.

Where did the bushy-tailed red squirrel go?

These dusty plains are this animal's home.

Where is he hiding? Where does he roam?

Is he lost in the tall waving grasses that grow?

Where did the broad-shouldered bison go?

Deep in the forests that stretch to the sky,

a mother and baby are hiding nearby.

Are they high in the mist or somewhere down low?

Where did the mountain gorillas go?

Up in the trees, so as not to be seen,

hangs a three-fingered creature with fur brownish-green.

You'll not see him move, for he's known to be slow —

where in the world did the sleepy sloth go?

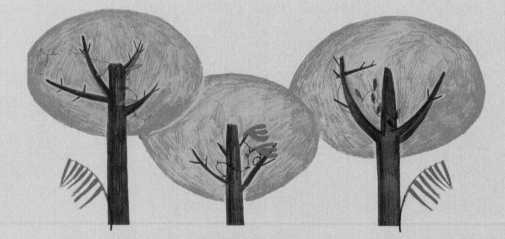

Someone is under the shady gum tree.

She has long pointed ears and a tail—can you see?

She digs in the earth to escape the sun's glow.

Where did the burrowing bilby go?

This slow, gentle reptile carries his home

around on his back in the shape of a dome.

Over the islands he plods to and fro.

Where did the giant tortoise go?

Someone with stripes of black and white

is trying to stay just out of sight.

But if you look closely, maybe she'll show.

Where did the galloping zebra go?

Someone is hunting on the Arctic ice floes.

He has thick fur and a little black nose.

He makes his home in this land of snow.

Where did the enormous polar bear go?

As day turns to night you may hear the howl

of this swift-footed hunter on the prowl.

She searches for food as the desert winds blow.

Where did the ghostly gray wolf go?

Who can you see when the wide river floods?

Is he deep in the water or down in the mud?

He searches for fish in the great river's flow.

Where did the snappy-nosed gharial go?

This big hungry bear loves

tall green bamboo.

She eats it all day;

how much can she chew?

She's somewhere close by with

black eyes and black toes.

Where did the round-bellied

giant panda go?

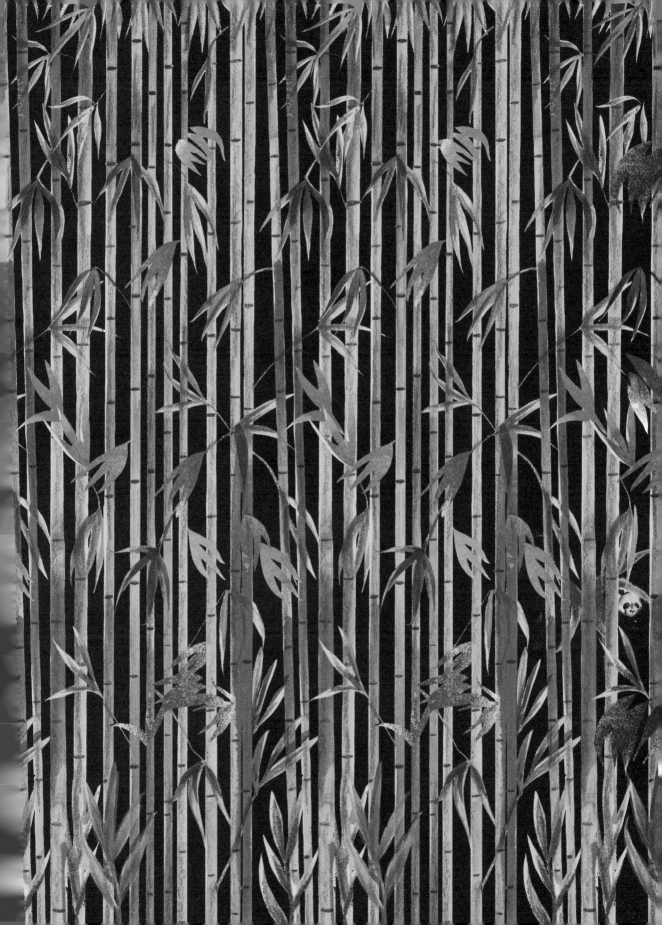

A snuffle, a snort, can be heard all about.

There's an animal here with a very long snout.

Off in the bushes, leaves are rustling so.

A tapir is near — just where did he go?

All around the world
in deserts and seas,
in mountains and rivers,
on land and in trees,
these creatures are hiding—
for how long we don't know.
What will become of them?
Where will they go?

Where did they go?

Did you find all the animals?

In the wild, many of them are very hard to find.

ADDAX

Addax used to be found throughout the Sahara Desert, but they are hunted for their horns and there are fewer than three hundred left in the wild.

MOUNTAIN GORILLA

Mountain gorillas are found high up in the thick forests of central and western Africa. These forests are being destroyed, and there are only around seven hundred mountain gorillas left.

RED SQUIRREL

Red squirrels are still common on mainland Europe, but the larger, stronger gray squirrels have almost completely replaced them in the United Kingdom.

SLOTH

Sloths move so slowly that sometimes algae grows on their fur! This provides camouflage in the rain forests of South and Central America where they live.

BISON

Bison can weigh more than a ton. Millions of them once roamed the grasslands of North America, but huge numbers were killed by nineteenth-century hunters.

BILBY

Bilbies are unique to Australia. Newborns stay in their mother's pouch until they are eleven weeks old. They are threatened by predators like foxes and cats, which have been introduced to the bilby's habitat.

GIANT TORTOISE

Giant tortoises live on the Galápagos Islands and weigh up to 550 pounds. They nearly became extinct when people brought egg-eating animals into their habitat.

GRAY WOLF

Gray wolves can hear one another howl from six to ten miles away. Mexican gray wolves are the smallest of all gray wolves and were hunted to near extinction in the United States.

ZEBRA

Grévy's zebras live across the savannas of eastern Africa. Each zebra has a unique pattern. More and more cattle are being grazed on the grasslands, leaving less food for zebra herds. They are also hunted for their skins.

GHARIAL

Gharials live in the rivers of the Indian subcontinent. They have more than one hundred razor-sharp teeth and long, thin snouts. Fewer than two hundred gharials may be left in the wild.

POLAR BEAR

Polar bears have adapted to live in the icy arctic. Under their thick fur they have black skin to soak in sunlight. They are threatened by warming oceans melting the ice on which they live and hunt.

GIANT PANDA

There are fewer than 2,000 giant pandas left. A panda can eat up to forty pounds of bamboo every day, but their bamboo forests are being cut down.

TAPIR

Malayan tapirs have lived in the Southeast Asian forests for millions of years, but are under threat from habitat loss. Tapirs have noses a little like an elephant's trunk.

To Mum, thank you for your never-ending support,
and to those who ensure all the endangered animals
in the world are protected

Text and design copyright © 2015 by The Templar Company Limited
Illustrations copyright © 2015 by Emily Bornoff

First U.S. edition 2016

Library of Congress Catalog Card Number pending
ISBN 978-0-7636-8920-9

16 17 18 19 20 21 TLF 10 9 8 7 6 5 4 3 2 1

Printed in Dongguan, Guangdong, China

This book was typeset in Brown.
The illustrations were created digitally.

BIG PICTURE PRESS
an imprint of
Candlewick Press
99 Dover Street
Somerville, Massachusetts 02144

www.candlewick.com
www.bigpicturepress.net